The World Is a Beautiful Place
Until It's Not!

By

Michelle Rogers

Copyright ©2022 Michelle Rogers

All rights reserved. No part of this publication may be reproduced, distributed, or transmitted in any form or by any means, including photocopying, recording, or other electronic or mechanical methods, without the prior written permission of the publisher, except in the case of brief quotations embodied in critical reviews and certain other noncommercial uses permitted by copyright law.

ISBN: 978-0-9891348-3-5

Liberation's Publishing – West Point - Mississippi

The World Is a Beautiful Place
Until It's Not!

Table of Content

The Words God Spoke to Me 9

Scattered Showers 10

I'm A Pretty Girl 12

I'm A Handsome Little Boy 13

More than That 14

The Town of Fakes 15

A Mother 16

Side Piece 18

Reevaluate Yourself 20

Missing 21

So You Thought 22

Do Black Lives Really Matter 23

Jealousy 24

Vows for Her 25

In The Arms of a Real Man 26

Love Without Being a Fool 27

Responding With Comfort 28

Relationships 29

Let It Be Known 30

Free You 31

Misunderstood Voice 32

The World Is a Beautiful Place 33

The Real Issue 34

Loosing A Child 36

Vows For Him 37

The Words You Speak Vs the Attention You Seek 38

Daddy Baby 39

Four Categories in One 40

Government Assistance 42

Anger with Rage 43

What's A Gun 44

Woman of Color 46

The Ugly Truth 47

A Night of Hurt 48

The Words God Spoke to Me

Don't concentrate on your thoughts

Just simply trust my plan and that you don't understand,

Just leave it in my hand

I am the truth and the life
Put all your trust in me
and everything will be alright.

Scattered Showers

As the sun shines bright scattered showers in the forecast and just like the roadrunner it came superfast

The brain is whole, thoughts over the place

Thinking it was rain until She noticed,

it was only the tears flowing down her face

One min the tears flow ... then stops ... to feeling ok.

She felt like a scattered shower just in a human way

Being broken, it hurts. Thinking but don't understand

But sometimes the things we go through are all a part of GODS plan,

Trying to Get our attention to let him lead us throughout the land.

The truth it can hurt, but the truth will set one free. The truth will even help you to view things for what it really be.

Loving unconditionally can sometimes cause pain

But with communication and humbleness understanding could be a gain.

On her face she refuses to show a frown, so she copes with the hurt with such a beautiful smile

Yet not understanding why ... the person she loved the most

was the one who let her down.

With tears in her eyes and the love in her heart

she builds herself to the woman she needs to be

while realizing the importance of her mind being at peace.

I'm A Pretty Girl

Looking in the mirror guess who I see, a pretty little girl
starring back at me

I'm a pretty little girl and respectful I'll be
I'm a pretty little girl with much success ahead of me

I'm a pretty little girl that's what everyone say
I'm a pretty little girl and I brighten my dad's day

I'm a pretty little girl no matter the color of my skin
I'm a pretty little girl with a big heart within

I'm a pretty little girl with such beautiful smile
And thanks to my mom for dressing me with style

I'm a pretty little girl and I'll strive for the best
I'm a pretty little girl and won't settle for less

I'm A Handsome Little Boy

Looking in the mirror guess who I see, a handsome little boy staring back at me.

I'm a handsome little boy, and respectful I'll be

I'm a handsome little boy with much success ahead of me.

I'm a handsome little boy that's what everyone says.

I'm a handsome little boy and I brighten my mom's day.

I'm a handsome little boy no matter the color of my skin

I'm a handsome little boy with a big heart within.

I'm a handsome little boy that will grow to be a man.

I'm a handsome little boy and for right I will stand.

I'm a handsome little boy and I'll strive for the best.

I'm a handsome little boy and will not settle for less.

More than That

When She's genuinely heard ... then She'll know ...
cause most men now days prove themselves to be a whore

Not caring about one's feelings, understanding or too much
of what they have to say

Just long as they get what they want no matter the hour of the
day

As a woman in life, she'll want much more and accepting
anything, she just can't do

her intentions are pure, her worth she knows, her time is
valuable, and her love is unconditional

She's different, yet rare, she's not a game to be played

She's a woman with self-respect not looking to just be laid

The Town of Fakes

They call the truth judging when in fact that's not the case,
it's just that the wrong person is speaking the truth, so they'll
say you're out your place

They love every inch of fake but it's the honesty they can't
take.

When speaking on others, their mouth opens to do
but when it hits home, lips sealed tight as if they used glue

In this town of fakes, a dictionary is what they need.
Cause a lot of words they use; they have no clue of what they
mean.

Sugarcoating ain't never been a thing for me to do
I've always been blunt along with speaking the truth.

Miss me with mess, when I'm only stating facts
Cause downing another is what I won't do.

Just take the responsibility, to stop speaking on others when
you have no room to.

A Mother

Having her own place and her own car to drive,
working two jobs, paying her bills, being the super mom
taking care of her kids.

Yes, she's independent, that's exactly what it is.

Being a mother comes with duties, what sense would it be to
complain.

Some days are tougher than others, but being strong a
mother remains

Homework, cooking, and cleaning
She does all of that too

She's a mother and by all means she does what she has to
do.

Giving love, showing support, and having a listening ear
forms a bond with your child to have a voice without fear.

Having your child's back, while letting them know when
they're wrong
helps them through the years and even when they are grown

A mother will never neglect her child to please a man.
A mother teaches respect while being the best example she
possibly can.

A mother protects her child and show them that she cares, and a mother if not dead will always be there.

Side Piece

You knew he had a woman, so what did you expect

He told you from the start all he wanted was some sex

You a sidepiece

Extra time you will not get

But you still were a fool letting your feelings get in the mix

Now depressed
going crazy
losing weight like you sick

Pull yourself together it ain't that serious bout some dick.

You a sidepiece and you should've played your role

Not cooking for a nigga trying to reach his soul

Stop blowing up his phone and stalking out his home,

You choose to be a sidepiece but should've left that alone

Understand your role so your heart don't be a wreck,

I got some advice hear me out for a sec.

Learning your place, and where you stand in someone's life

Will save you disappointments
And the feeling of not being treated right

Time is valuable it should not become a waste

If you don't know where you stand that just might be the case.

But why be a sidepiece when you're in fact the whole meal

Your everything plus
So, half love, no deal

Why be a sidepiece confusing lust for love?

You're a woman so let no man place you under and not above!!

Reevaluate Yourself

She wants a man
not a boy that'll only play with her heart
not realizing she shouldn't dress as if she's a shopping mart

Her man has to have a good job
cause she loves all the fancy gifts,
she works, but cooking and cleaning ... her hand she doesn't lift

She say she need a man that don't have such a long criminal sheet,
But ask yourself are you a woman that a real man will be pleased to meet?

She says "my face is darn Gorgeous, and My body is banging hot"
Don't address me like a whore, and don't look at me like a thot"
not realizing her actions is saying an awful lot

Looks are good, dressing nice is too,
your sex can be great!!

But Those are material things that ain't hard to find
but a real man needs a woman that's well worth his time.

Missing

With you .... Her hearts' a float, A float for far too long

It's the days She feel uncomfortable, unwanted and all alone

At times she feels your love
and sometimes she don't ...
be honest is she really, the woman you truly want?

She loves herself that's how she's able to love you
She explains the way she feel... but the heck with that too.

Sometimes she move like the weak,
Although she really is strong ...

Her problem is people viewing her as the person that's in the wrong

She's missable
Nonreplaceable
Be careful what you put her through
Cause when she gone, she's gone,
There's No coming back to you 💔 🤙

If you choose not to support, show love and be her man respectfully remove yourself so a real gentleman can ‼️

So You Thought

The social media life he's the man of every woman's dream

Positive speaker, standup guy, He's an inspirational king

With the perfect words to say on honor and respect

But the man behind closed doors is the one you haven't meet

He's Being a man to the world and that's absolutely no way to be especially if being a man is nothing I the wife see

He Declines on the help that he sees and knows I need but feels obligated to a stranger in doing a good deed

It's not that guys don't want the person they're with some are just doggish, wanting every woman they can get

You can't look at social media and think you have the truth

I was the wife sitting back watching how he was making a fool of you

Warnings come first I explained to get him to see but he didn't understand till the day he was missing me

Though you thought it was cute and even called me weak

Those words you proudly sowed rest for sure you will reap ‼

Do Black Lives Really Matter

Black Lives Matter how can that be when black on black crimes is what I yet see

Black Lives Matter that's what they say, while shooting each other down in the streets they lay

Black Lives Matter in fact that's true Black Lives Matter and blacks should understand that too

Blacks killing blacks, no killing is nothing to gain just leaving family members in heartache and pain

My black people when will you learn everybody ain't hating some are truly concerned

Everybody ain't judging in reality stating facts, and when speaking the truth some hate to accept that

My black people why can't you get along instigating stupidity 10 minutes later on, it's long live C I can't believe he gone

Black Lives Matter is what you want everyone to see take a minute to ask yourself "do black lives really matter to me "

When blacks come together treat and care for one another right

When blacks come together in choosing peace over a fight

When blacks come together and work as team again my black people will elevate as a whole and start to win.

Jealousy

Jealousy is a drug that no one needs.

Jealousy can be a drug that'll make an innocent person bleed.

Sometimes family and the people we call friends,

Be the main ones praying on our success to end.

I've heard move in silence which ain't a bad thing to do.

Cause the ones you think not be the ones to envy you.

Being Successful without a diploma or degree will have a jealous heart questioning "why them and not me."

Jealousy has people purchasing things they can't truly afford but find it hard to congratulate someone on their achievement award.

Some meet their goals before others do be happy not jealous Let it motivate you.

GOD made us all different but gave us all a chance at life.

The things that others have, is not always for you

Be content with your own life, GOD will deliver the blessings he has in-store for you.

Vows for Her

She a blessing from God

That's clear to see

God's beautiful creation that he placed here just for me

Trust me with your heart I'm not like the rest and with all in me I'll give you the best

Taking you in my care it's to love and protect and as a real gentleman I will always give you respect

Your every sparkle in my eye you're the icing to my cake and whenever I hurt, you're the cure to my ache

Until the end of time you'll be the person I adore so thankful I was heard because your everything I prayed for...

In The Arms of a Real Man

In the arms of a real man, he accepts you for who you are but at the same time he gives motivation in all positive things you do and along with a real man comes respect and loyalty too.

In the arms of a real man intentions are pure, and if it takes going the extra mile, he makes sure his woman feel secure.

What he speaks become actions his love you'll definitely feel if he found you with a broken heart be prepared for it to heal

In the arms of a real man your mind is at peace and in return he needs a woman that's gone also bring him peace

A real man needs a woman that's gone stand by his side and someone he can show off with much dignity and pride

In the arms of a real man, he knows exactly what you need and also, he has the knowledge to properly lead

When dealing with a real man you can't always think on you cause respect, loyalty and love a real man needs that too.

Love Without Being a Fool

Can you look at your significant other and see the love upon their face

Love is a beautiful thing when it's actions to what you say

Love is a bond that's created between two

And love will not be so quick to give up on you

Love is not abuse love don't cheat love should be one thing that brings you peace

patience is love not meaning be a fool

when you love you'll be surprised of the things you accept and do

fight for who you love, know when to be through and stop loving people more than you love you

Responding With Comfort

I know it hurt your heart the day Your child departed earth, keep in mind of the memories from the moment of birth

If there was anything you could do, I know for your child you would have been there to rescue

Don't beat yourself up there was nothing you could have done

Just do her one huge favor by holding to heart the special bond

I know it don't seem fair, but
GOD don't put no more on us than what we can bare

Though your child is not here in body its pictures you can yet see

She was A young black entrepreneur The G.O.A.T how they described her to me

Sometimes you may sit and stare into space take time and visualize the beautiful smile worn upon her face

Family, Friends, siblings, mom and Dad Remember your special loved one by the love and Joy she had...

Relationships

Sometimes in Relationships things come to an end
And some build a lasting bond while positioning each other in ways to win

Relationships sometimes can move to fast just as well in some relationships they move to slow

Relationships can be based on so many different things be wise way it out before giving or receiving a wedding ring

In relationships Honesty, love, respect, communication and loyalty too plays a huge part believe me for that is true

Some women can have a good man and want to appreciate some men can have a good woman and won't realize until it's too late

In a relationship in my opinion, it shouldn't be a limit on spending time cause me I'm clingy and like to cuddle under what's mine

Never base your relationship on what other relationships have or do cause what you see on the outside could be a struggle and or ain't always true

Two people can be compatible but that doesn't mean they belong understand me when I say no one can break up your happy home

For No relationship you see is perfect let no one deceive you and always respect your own relationship before expecting someone else too

Let It Be Known

When lying and cheating seems all you know to do how can you speak on loyalty when being loyal ain't apart of you

Communication and understanding is great for the mind, heart and soul but how can you enlighten someone else when it's so easy for you to fold

Communication you never have time understanding ain't really trying to but when the tables turn you want everyone to talk and understand you

How can a married man speak on how he loves his wife when sexually he's trying to enter another woman's life

If negative traits of you is all I see, how can you possibly speak positive to me

When women teach boys it's from a woman's point of view that's why when some grow up, they do things of a woman too

A woman can raise a boy she can't teach him to be a man but why is that so hard for some to understand

So many people have so many great things to say but observing their actions they match no kind of way...

Free You

The feeling of wanting to rescue but it ain't nothing I can do, my heart ache, my head hurt thinking why it had to be you

The moment of reading your name I said this just can't be, cause well-mannered and respectful you were all that to me

I'll accept it when I see proof or when it's said by you cause right now in my heart, I don't believe it's true

A long life ahead… I hope I'm right on this … living in the free world I pray you don't have to miss

I know that lives were taken and I'm not justifying wrong but to think you pulled a trigger I just feel like they are wrong

I hope you have an alibi to prove where you was at, I tell you it breaks my heart to see your name in the mix of that

I pray your name is cleared so you can return home, but in the meantime young man stay strong.

Misunderstood Voice

What's life without life living but feeling dead

Believe it or not that thought comes across my head

Asking myself daily why do I live cause when I speak, I'm misunderstood, and being disrespectful was all they say I give

Not so much of disrespect more of when people see that your smart and happy with a glow, they'll do all they can to break you down low

Depression is real I've been there before

Ending my on life I've came so close to do, thanking GOD for being GOD and bringing me through

My kids heart aching cause of my face they no longer see I couldn't imagine my kids living their life without me.

Today I stand stronger than I was on that day and learned not to accept nor listen to the negative that people have to say

With life We never know but GOD knows it all and when You don't know the words to say GOD is the one you can always call

GOD know our hearts and the words we're trying to say even when people which it up to make it seem another way

misunderstood by people walking this earth I've learned and reminding you just keep GOD first ♥

The World Is a Beautiful Place

Riding in my car the windows down feeling a cool breeze while viewing what's around

A light blue sky, white clouds that seem to move, tall green trees and different cars passing by

Hearing birds chirp seeing the sun shine bright puts a glow on my view and sun kissed just right 😊

In a deep train of thought my mind takes a turn to think of the different things that's taken place

How goals are being meet, houses being built, couples getting married
sick people being healed

kids being molested and or neglected, innocent people being killed not given a chance to live

Funds running low, people losing their mind, jobs closing down, just extra chaos all around

The world was made such a beautiful place, it's just bad things that's taken place stay in line with GOD so he can lend your way

Cause Despite the things go on and the different battles we face the world in my eyes is yet a beautiful place 🖤

The Real Issue

In this world today with all the crazy things that go on it's some of the older individuals that want admit when they are wrong

Blaming every fault on the young bashing them all as a whole but just because it's one don't make them all out of control

Everyone see the reaction, but no one see the cause a lot of you older thugs are the reason for it all

A lot of older people say they wasn't like the generation today, but truth be told some are the reason the young is corrupt this way

Old heads use to sit back and give the youngsters drugs to sell and let them know if they got caught keep they mouth and not to tell

Some of the old heads actually pass knowledge and teach the young respect and encourage them to attend college

The older Drinking, smoking and chopping it up right with the young when in fact from the older the young is supposed to learn so as they get older what do you expect them to do when they sat around as a younger child seeing and hearing everything you went to do

Coming from old head calling the young a "straight hoe No heart" lets me know he wasn't a man when it came to doing his part

You can forever bash the young and not accept the fact but a lot of the violence today an older head is responsible for that

Older heads woman or man lets go about this a much different way by speaking life and positive things into our youth each and every day 🖤

Loosing A Child

Asking GOD for strength, I didn't know what to do

Wasn't ready by far the day I lost you

The unbearable hurt cause there was nothing I could do

My child My child I'm lost without you.

Not knowing what to think, and not wanting to question why

I can't believe my baby … took wings and halo for the sky

Rest on my love life and death we're apart but I'll forever keep you close and dear to my heart...

Vows For Him

Your everything to me in every single way

It's the love you prove for me day by day

Your Interest for me haven't failed yet after four years it's the same from the moment we meet

I love and respect you for the man you are and always have been and I'll definitely have your back through thick and thin

We had our ups and down which every relationship do most importantly I'm thankful we're able to talk things through

Asking for my hand in marriage nearly took my breath away but spending the rest of life with you I wouldn't have it any other way

I've been trusting you with my heart as you do with me, and I promise to be the best wife God created me to be.

The Words You Speak Vs the Attention You Seek

Demanding respect with the words they say Begging for attention any possible way

Dressing in ways to show everything they got, and have the nerve to get mad when addressed as a Thot

Riding they own wave is what they claim to do, but heavy on following, doing what others do

So Quick to say Don't disrespect me next min they hollering I'mma bad B!

Self-love is the best love, a statement that's felt but why so easy to disrespect self

Have you ever noticed the females that call themselves a bad B! Don't keep no man long enough for anyone to see

Let some tell it they deserve much better but on Facebook discussing how to make them wetter

Take her to the bed she'll open her legs, turn on some music she'll twerk to the end, but take her to the kitchen she don't know where to begin

the way you speak vs the attention you seek

Stop thinking with your bodies and other material things find self-respect and one day you'll meet your king!!

Daddy Baby

Little girl, you will always and forever have my heart 🩶

Daddy baby, so beautiful, genuine, and smart

From birth you've always ment a lot to me

My little girl, to your daddy you'll always be.

In life situations can get a lil rough but I'm your daddy and for fact I know you built tough

But if any situation for you ever get to hard call on your daddy, your personal bodyguard 🗿

My little girl, I'm your number one fan

And daddy gone always do what He can

Some things I might not be able to do, but daddy will always and forever love you

Four Categories in One

Reading comments on a post, talking about the news
they say the young generation is messed up but the comments
I'm confused

Out the mouth of an older lady Speaking negative over and
about the young

The lesson she taught that quick was to throw stone for stone

Riot in hell, throw them away, with all the other filthy things
they say

Makes me wonder if it was their child would they still choose
those words to say

Passing judgment destroying characters before knowing the
facts of any case

So many young lives at state and sadly some have passed
away

But how could Anyone have known it was the wrong crowd,
time and place

"The younger generation is gone"
That's what I hear folks say

But what about the older heads that supply guns for the
young anyway!!

that's a statement some older heads hate elaborating on today

Serval tongues need to get still and lips need to be sealed

especially if you're not gone speak positive and pray for the land to heal

Cause some of the things you speak your manifesting in the land today, that's why it's so important to be mindful of the things you say!! 🎯

To any family that's going through I pray strength, comfort and understanding too, Cause The loss of someone you love is never easy for anyone

And From the bottom my heart I pray your days get bright and your heaviness get light keep trusting in GOD and everything will be alright 🖤

Government Assistance

She's lazy, but clocking in for work you didn't want to do

"She get food stamps", That's right, don't let that bother you

Downing the car I drive thinking it would hurt me imma drive it like a 21 even though it's 03 she a bad mamma Jama getting me everywhere I need to be

My rent only ten dollars, at least that's what you say, but rest for sure it's not eight hundred the rent you can barely pay

Saying things you thought, would embarrass me,
But you gotta come a lil stronger other than speaking on my teeth

You say you make more money than I'll ever make doing hair... but as long as you make your money why would my money to you even care

Remember the money you borrowed from me, in order to fix your nails but I'm poor, government assistance to the next you'll tell

Anger with Rage

With air blowing in my face my eyes burning with rage
anger and past hurts trapped in my body like it's a cage

Silent screams you can't hear, but on my face the anger
appear

My throat forms a knot, the anger explodes, and in my hand
if anything I release wherever it goes

Hyperventilation and the shaking of my leg a delay when I
speak but meaning every word I said

I say that I don't care with
With tears rolling down my face I'm thankful GOD saw fit
to yet shower me with his grace

People I thought so much of opening up about self always
showed me how much they didn't care

Tension in my neck thoughts to "just wreck, rage to the most
high, Realizing it was Satan instructing me in a way to die

Anger and rage I don't like how it make me feel, lord
remove it all is my daily prayer to heal

I write things on paper to
Clear my mind and soul but Today I needed GOD to take
total control

What's A Gun

A gun in your hands don't make you tough

A gun in some hands when scared it's not for bluff

Thinking it's cool but don't fully understand

Guns and drugs both slowly destroying the land

innocent people not targeted but their lives being taken away

parents hurt, angry, and speechless not knowing what to think or say

Loose guns, cross fire bullets moving through the air, the person Behind the gun shooting without a single care

Where do a mind be and what exactly do they think in the streets it's not man but a male that's pink

blaming it all on the young and their insane acts, speaking on it all day but reaching out is where you lack

Some need love some just reprobated some missing fathers if not dead incarcerated

Some of the young raised right but the music they hear they scared at heart but with a Gun it's nothing they fear

A gun don't make you a man, that's what some needs to know, walking off don't make you weak it saves you from being shot down like a dog in the street

What's a gun in any hand When it's a loose hand that shoot, taking life's they didn't give or had any reason too

STOP all the violence and START to show more love cause with some individuals all they need is caring hug..

Try having a listening ear to whoever needs you but also encourage them on something positive to do

There's consequences to pay and justifying wrong no way so before you pull a trigger ask yourself .. is it really worth me throwing my life away ...

Woman of Color

I'm a woman of color that's in love with my skin

I'm woman of color that's destined to win

I'm a woman of color made beautiful you see, take a moment don't rush.... Don't you agree?

Even if you don't I yet know so cause when I look into the mirror on my face a beautiful glow

I'm a woman of color independent and strong finding my way and taking care of my home

I'm a woman of color that has a big heart a even bigger brain that has me wealthy and smart

If I stumble and fall I'll get up and stand tall

Cause I'm a woman of color and I'll succeed at it all

Not to be cocky just speaking the truth I'm a woman of color that's blunt and humble too .

The Ugly Truth

Keeping my mouth closed on certain ways I feel no more will I ever keep my lips sealed

Love you for what when you gave me no reason to care for you why when caring for me ain't what you do

Some guys will use you up till you can't be used again then move to the next woman thinking he up for a win

Being a good woman doing everything you know to do ain't never been a reason to make a man want you

Doing wifely duties before you actually become the wife is one of the biggest mistakes you can ever make in life

Some guys are very sneaky they'll suck your pockets dry while having what they need and yet they still lie

When it comes to Older guys you would think they have sense however some are very childish and at this point shouldn't exist

It may have sounded harsh but it wasn't my plan to sometimes that's what it takes just speak the ugly truth

A Night of Hurt

In a relationship and yet feeling alone

Notice the red flags to know when something is wrong

Crying In silence some nights till You fall asleep

It's a hurt that's none forgettable cause it cuts you really deep

A thin line of communication not so much of a bond

Memories are like fishing for fish out an empty pond

I'm stuck between my heart and what I actually feel my mind and how I think, to the things I accept and the love I give

Not that I'm stupid nor am I weak but love plays a huge part when it's something you seek ..

Tears may flow due to the way you feel, get in the mix with GOD that way your heart can begin to heal 🖤

www.ingramcontent.com/pod-product-compliance
Lightning Source LLC
Chambersburg PA
CBHW011614290426
44110CB00020BA/2587